Tuning In

Clay Creatures should be read from s[tart]
secure the idea that instructions follo[w]
need to be read in order. It may be h[elpful]
the children make one of the models

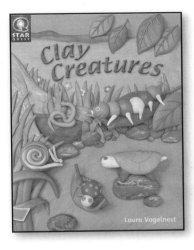

The front cover

Let's read the title together.

Look at the front cover. What do you think the picture has been made from?

What creatures can you see?

The back cover

What does the blurb tell us?

This is an instruction book that tells you how to make things from clay.

What other instructions can you think of?

Contents

Introduction	2
Make a Ball	4
Make a Pancake	5
Make a Rope	6
Make a Caterpillar	7
Make a Turtle	11

Contents

Instruction books have a contents page. This one tells you the different things that you can make and helps you to find information on different pages.

Have any of you made clay creatures before?

READ

Read pages 2 and 3

Purpose: to find out what you will need and to recognize that this is a standard way of starting instructions.

PAUSE

Pause at page 3

What materials will you need to get before you can start?

Who can read the sentence that tells us?

What shapes will we need to use when we make clay creatures?

Introduction

You will need:

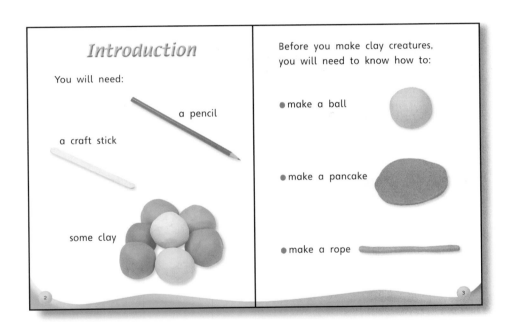

a pencil

a craft stick

some clay

Before you make clay creatures,
you will need to know how to:

● make a ball

● make a pancake

● make a rope

READ

Read page 4

Purpose: to recognize the heading and 'read' the information in the photographs.

PAUSE

Pause at page 4

What does the heading say?

Why is the heading in large letters?

How do you make a ball?

What do the photographs tell us?

READ

Read page 5

Purpose: to look at the language of instructions.

PAUSE

Pause at page 5

Who can read the words that tell us what order to do things in? (*first, then*)

Which words tell us what to do? (*make, press, smooth*)

Let's read the last sentence together.

Make a Ball

Roll the clay round and round between your hands to make a ball.

4

Make a Pancake

First make a ball. Then press the ball down. Make it flat like a pancake. Smooth out any cracks.

6

READ

Read page 6

Purpose: to find out how to make a rope.

PAUSE

Pause at page 6

What are you going to make now?

How do you make the rope?

What do you have to do to make the rope longer and thinner?

READ

Read page 7

Purpose: to find out how to make a caterpillar.

PAUSE

Pause at page 7

What is this going to be? Can you find the word 'caterpillar'?

What do you make first?

How do you make the balls stick together?

How many balls would *you* make?

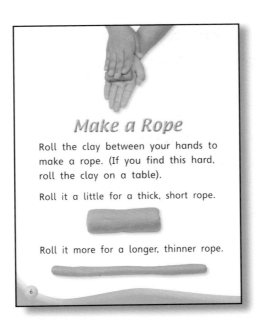

Make a Rope

Roll the clay between your hands to make a rope. (If you find this hard, roll the clay on a table).

Roll it a little for a thick, short rope.

Roll it more for a longer, thinner rope.

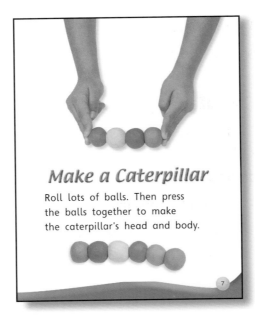

Make a Caterpillar

Roll lots of balls. Then press the balls together to make the caterpillar's head and body.

READ

Read pages 8 and 9

Purpose: to understand the purpose of each element in the instructions.

PAUSE

Pause at page 9

What are the balls for?

Why do the eyes need two different colours?

How do you use the pencil?

Why do you need a craft stick?

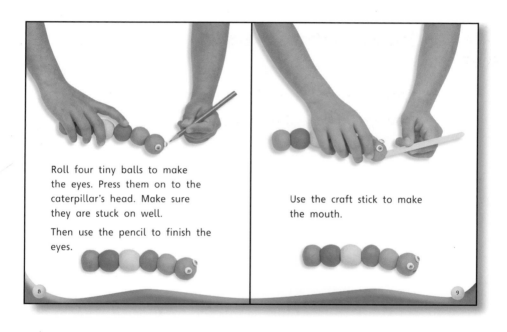

Roll four tiny balls to make the eyes. Press them on to the caterpillar's head. Make sure they are stuck on well.

Then use the pencil to finish the eyes.

Use the craft stick to make the mouth.

READ

Read page 10

Purpose: to recall the sequence for making a caterpillar.

PAUSE

Pause at page 10

What are the last things you need to do to finish the caterpillar?

Who can remember what order you make things in?

(Praise the children who use 'first', 'next', and 'then' in their recall.)

READ

Read page 11

Purpose: to understand what to make next.

PAUSE

Pause at page 11

Why is 'Make a Turtle' in large print?

What are the first words in each sentence?

Why do you make a pancake?

How many legs has a turtle?

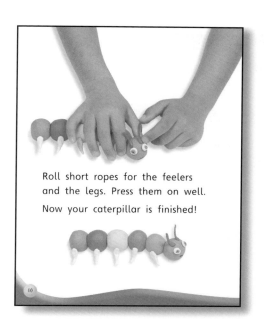

Roll short ropes for the feelers
and the legs. Press them on well.

Now your caterpillar is finished!

Make a Turtle

Make a pancake for the turtle's shell.
Then roll four short ropes for the legs.

READ

Read pages 12 and 13

Purpose: to look at the order and language of instructions.

PAUSE

Pause at page 13

What do you make after the legs?

What do you need for the turtle's tail?

What do you do next?

What is missing from the turtle?

Roll a longer, thick rope for the turtle's head. Then roll a shorter, thin rope for the tail.

Press the head, tail and legs under the shell. Press them on well.

READ

Read pages 14 and 15

Purpose: to recognize the start and end of a sentence.

PAUSE

Pause at page 15

How many sentences are there on page 14?

What must you do when you come to a full stop?

How do you make the eyes for the turtle?

What do you use to make the mouth?

READ

Read page 16

Purpose: to identify the creatures and think about the sequence for making them.

PAUSE

Pause at page 16

Who can name the creatures on this page?

How do you make a worm?

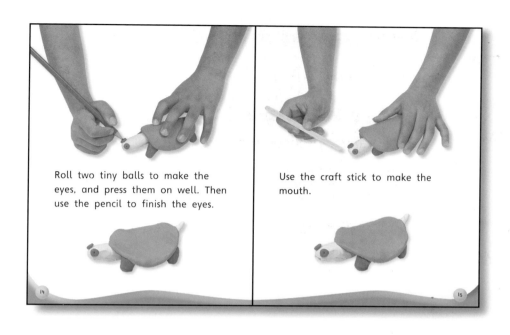

Roll two tiny balls to make the eyes, and press them on well. Then use the pencil to finish the eyes.

Use the craft stick to make the mouth.

What other creatures can you make?

After Reading

Revisit and Respond

T What was the sequence for making a turtle?

T Which creature would you like to make? (If possible, allow the children to follow the instructions and make some clay creatures themselves.)

S Look at page 6. What different punctuation marks can you see? (*commas, full stops, capital letters*)

W Look at the instruction words 'first', 'then', 'press', 'make', 'finish'. Let's see if we can write the words from memory.